GREATNESS IN A NUTSHELL

Doreyl Ammons Cain

Seat of your Pants
VISUAL MEDIA

10 Joy Lane • Waynesville, North Carolina 28786

Cover Art & Illustrations- Doreyl Ammons Cain
Edited by- Amy Ammons Garza
Layout & Typography- Jerry Cain

Published by *Seat of Your Pants Visual Media*
10 Joy Lane • Waynesville, North Carolina 28786
Website: http://www.soyplogos.com

Revised Edition

ISBN 0-9668900-2-7

For the Creative Spirit
in all People

-Forward-

Twenty years ago I opened my small design and advertising agency in Southern California. With a specialty in business logo and image development, I set out to change the world with my designs. This step became one of the most self-fulfilling moments of my life. The time was right and the agency grew like wildfire. Within two years I had a sales, creative and design staff of ten people, with two large retainer accounts and twenty small accounts. The business exploded--exciting, creative and challenging.

It's true that if you have a dream and believe in it, you can do it. Throughout my years in marketing design I observed new business owners who truly understood their purpose, accomplish their dream. After understanding comes action. The first step is creating a visual representation of your dream; a logo. Eye-catching graphic identity for your business is crucial for its long term success. Psychologists say that we remember one/fifth of what we hear, two/fifths of what we see, and four /fifths of everything we see and hear at the same time. Your ideas become tangible and alive when they are represented with a visual symbol containing *both* art and words that effectively communicate your message.

"Greatness in a Nutshell" guides you through the process of creating or recreating your logo and using it in an expansive way. If you have a dream or new idea , this book can help you more clearly communicate your purpose, vision and mission. With "Greatness in a Nutshell" you can find your position in the global marketplace, understand your niche, and learn how to better communicate your ideas to your target market . The " icing on the cake" is finally creating a symbol that truly represents the quality and uniqueness of your special endeavor, so that your dream will develop and prosper.

Contents

Introduction

In the early 90's I traveled from the Blue Ridge Mountains, across the Piedmont farming country, through Raleigh, to the Outer Banks of North Carolina conducting small business marketing workshops. I was filled with enthusiasm and earnestly wanted to spread the idea that when you *follow your dream, prosperity will follow you.* After spending twenty years in free-lance design and running a design & marketing firm in Southern California I had a lot to say.

The highlight of the workshops was the "Vision & Mission" section. We would go through a process to focus on the purpose of each participant's business and it always turned out to be something different than what they believed. Most small business owners thought they were simply in business to make money. One man in particular stands out in my mind. The location happened to be at a small business center in a metropolitan area of Coastal North Carolina. Many of the sixty participants were directors of nonprofit organizations with worthwhile missions, or dedicated owners of small service businesses.

Each person stood up, looking for the right words to describe their careers and businesses. The group had been instructed to listen carefully so they could help with constructing a fitting mission statement for their fellow participant. A man, quiet through most of the workshop, stood up and spoke.

" I am the owner of a strip show bar located on the beach."

We all looked at one another.
In a hesitant voice he continued, *"It's been in my family for years, my father owned it before me."*

I began to question him, *" How do you feel about your business? Does it bring you fulfillment?"*

He hesitated a few moments and then thoughtfully replied, *"I know the stress most business people are under. When they come to my place, most of it disappears. I figure when people can have a nice place to relax and have fun, they will live a longer, happier life."*

After a moment someone spoke, *"So your business purpose is to supply a relaxing stress-free environment for business people."*

The man said, *"Yes"* and seemed extremely relieved as he sat down.

The initial judgement of the group about the man's business had disappeared from the room and I knew it was going to be an unforgettable learning experience as a workshop facilitator.

Before a logo for any endeavor can be designed, the purpose, vision and mission must be clearly understood. This is the foundation for graphic image development, promotional materials, strategic and marketing plans. After reading this book and completing the creative processes, you will be able to have a more confident and realistic view of your future.

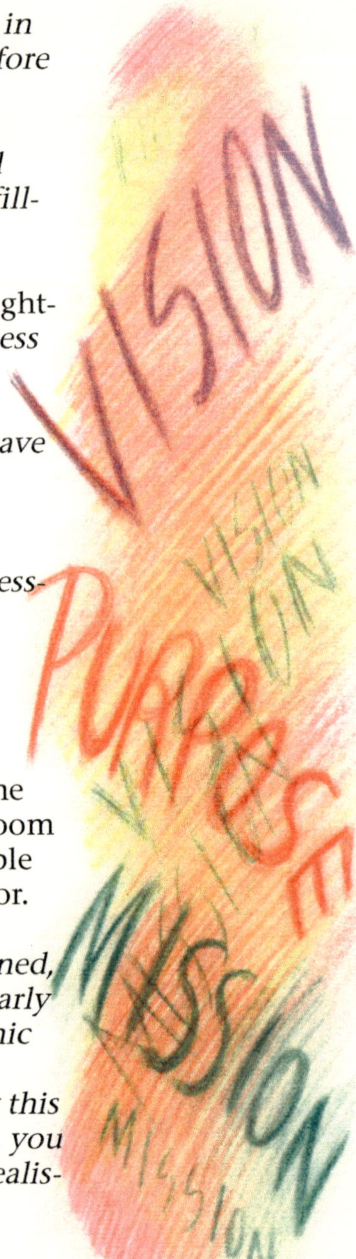

Chapter One

The Essence Of You

" Confidence, courage and commitment comes through clarity of purpose"

At the core of an apple rests seeds for future growth. To find the seeds you must peel away the outside skin and carve away the fruit until the core is exposed. Throughout this chapter we will be peeling away the surface ideas you have about your purpose and getting to the central theme that truly runs your organization. Like the man who owned the strip show bar that had been in his family for generations, your purpose is not always what it seems on the surface. His purpose, which he discovered through the "Vision and Mission" workshop, is "to supply a relaxing, stress-free environment for business people." Even though this particular format, a strip show, was his family's accepted way to accomplish his purpose, there are many other ways to do so. As an example, we will be examining many avenues for him to widen his horizons throughout this book.

Most people think that you go into business to make money, bottom line. It is obviously very important to make a living at whatever you are doing, but why did you pick this particular type of profession to spend enormous amounts of time and energy? If the work is not emotionally rewarding, your health, relationships and eventually your financial rewards will suffer. There is a basic, core idea behind your work that is the flavoring of everything you accomplish. This idea is extremely important and rewarding to you. The following processes will help you become clear about your purpose.

Now, let's take a look at your endeavor....

PURPOSE

Phase I

Your Purpose

*Year*________

Complete the following as quickly as you can:

1. Describe your work using adjectives that include color, size, shape, texture, etc.

Find a quiet place where you can comfortably write. Begin this process by clearing your mind of the "normal" way you perceive your work. Look at it as if you were describing something you are holding in your hand.

2. Describe the reason you started your particular work.

3. What need does your endeavors serve?

4. Describe, in detail, the people who benefit from your product and/or service.

5. How are your ideas different from others in your field?

6. What "niche" do you fit into?

6. Do you know where you fit in the global marketplace? Describe.

7. What is most personally gratifying about your work?

8. Write a sentence describing your professional purpose.*

**A purpose statement is the core essence of any endeavor. It states who, what, where and why.*

Phase II

Seeing a picture of what's possible

Your purpose statement is written. The next step is to create a vision for your future. Based on a clear purpose statement you can visualize the kind of future that is most probable and desirable. (Before we go on, do you feel clear and comfortable about your professional purpose? If not, please repeat phase I until you reach clarity.)

Visualization is the act of "seeing a picture" of what's possible in the present and/or future. You can "visualize" in various ways. One way is to "actually see" what can happen. When you are able to do this you can describe what you see with words, and/or actually draw a picture of the scene in your mind. In the "Vision & Mission" workshop many participants have stated emphatically that they could not visualize or draw. Yet during this visualization process they have created full color drawings of what they "see."

For example, an Alcohol & Drug Rehabilitations projects director for a Native American tribe organization sketched a picture that included a full landscape. Her drawing showed young people working together with animals, plants and Elders in a green valley, dotted with trees and flowers, nestled between hazy blue mountains. The drawing was clear, detailed and filled with harmony. She could hardly believe she had created her picture and did not know from where it came. After four years this vision is now becoming a reality in the form of a Native American Culture Center where the children can learn about their roots and environment through the Elders.

Other workshop participants have sketched highly detailed drawings of a day care center, an animal boarding facility, an art center and other long term projects that until the workshop, they were unable to visualize.

Another way to record what you "see" is to write down what your vision "feels like," "sounds like," or what you see yourself accomplishing in the next ten years.

The Process

1. See yourself in your place of work. What are you doing?

With this book and colored pencils close by, find a comfortable place, close your eyes and relax for about ten minutes. If your mind remains busy, focus on your breathing. Breath in deeply, breath out slowly, until your mind is clear of unceasing chatter.
Once you are relaxed and free of busy thoughts, begin to write answers to the following questions. Write as fast as you can.

2. Describe how your work makes you feel. Do you feel passionate about your work?

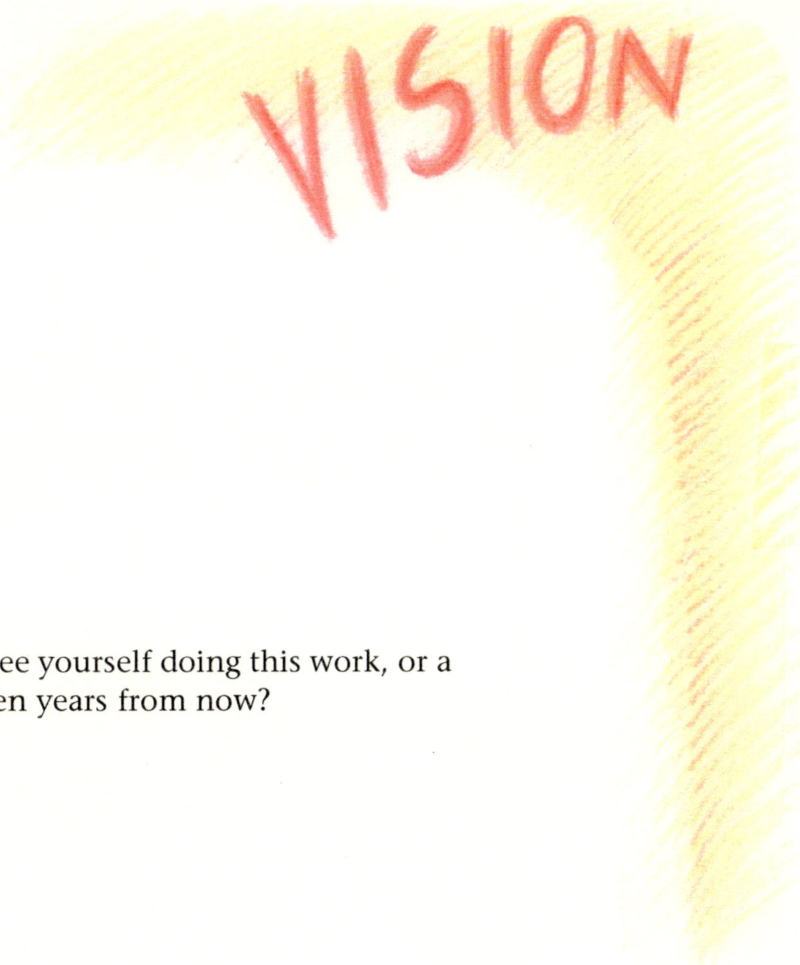

3. Can you see yourself doing this work, or a form of it, ten years from now?

4. What does your work look like? In ten years how have things changed in your work environment?

5. With colored pencils sketch what you see:

6. Do you see any problems with your picture of the future?

Take a moment and list any foreseeable problems:

7. What can you do now to prevent these problems?

8. Describe how your vision benefits your customers and the global marketplace?

9. Now, place your vision sketch in front of you. In one sentence, write your ten year vision statement based on what you see.

Make a copy of your vision statement and your drawing and place them where you can see them every day. Rip up your list of problems and forget them, you must concentrate on your vision

Phase III
Mastering the Mission

How do you start down the road to reach your vision? The first step is taken through the process of creating a mission statement.

How is a mission statement different from a purpose or vision statement? A purpose statement defines your endeavor, a vision is a picture of your future and a mission is the steps taken to get you there. A mission statement leads your action steps in a direct line towards your vision. Action steps are goals you set and/or signposts to let you know where you are along the way.

To stay focused, ask yourself "Will this action bring me closer to my vision?" A mission statement is ever changing, adjusting to what's happening along your vision pathway.

Make yourself comfortable, relax and clear your mind. Focus on your breath. When you feel free of mind chatter, write the answer to these questions as quickly as possible.

The Process

1. What can I do today to make my vision a reality?

2. What can I do everyday to make my vision a reality?

3. List the most logical steps you can take to begin your journey:

4. Prioritize the steps in item 3 in the order of importance and timing.

5. Write in one sentence a mission statement for your endeavor.

You now have a clear purpose, vision and mission statement. This gives a valuable platform to design a renewed marketing plan for your further improvement and success.

Chapter Two

Where Do You Fit?

"It Takes Trust to Build a Dream"

In the film "Field of Dreams," location was everything. The phrase, "Build it, and they will come." filled the minds and imagination of all who saw this creative film. The story is about a man who risked everything to build a big league baseball diamond in a corn field behind his house. His friends and community thought he was "nuts."

It takes faith to build. It also takes courage to step forward based on your intangible ideas. This next process will help you build trust. You now have a good grasp of the essence of your work; it's time to look at where you fit in the marketplace. The ideal location is where you can maximize your business with the least amount of effort. This location is the most convenient place for those you serve.

McDonalds hamburger chain is a good example. McDonalds saw a need for fast food in a growing American trend where both husband and wife work outside the home. They placed their fast food establishments in a convenient location for families to stop in and then created an eye-catching logo everyone could easily remember--The Golden Arches. They saw a need, filled it, made it convenient, clean and attractive.

Now, let's take a look at your field of dreams....

The Process

1. Where are you located in your vision for the future? Describe the place.

With purpose, vision and mission in front of you, make yourself comfortable and relax. Let yourself see, feel or hear the answers to the questions.

2. In your vision location, who are you serving? Describe the people.

3. Look around you. Who is in the same field of business? Describe them.

4. What is it about your endeavor and its location that best serves the needs of your customers and the global community?

5. Why is your location important to you?

6. Write, in one sentence, where you fit in the global community.

Finding your niche is one of the keys that opens the door to prosperity. The journey of finding "where you fit" brings you closer. The next chapter focuses on what makes you different and how your uniqueness is a valuable asset when it comes to "niche marketing."

Chapter Three

What Makes You Different?

"We are all valuable gifts, as varied as the leaves that fall in Autumn, a cascade of many colors, values and hues."

I remember sitting in front of a fireplace, high in the Smoky Mountains of North Carolina, watching my Grandfather carve a donkey out of soft birch wood. The light of the fire shone on his strong chin, weathered face and the clear blue of his eyes. A crippled Appalachian man, Grandpa made his living carving axe handles and, at times distilling moonshine. To me, he was a "one of a kind." I'll never forget his stories about growing up in those rugged mountains in the early 1900's. Although he's gone now, I'll remember him always with pleasure.

What makes us remember people and places? Take a moment and remember, in detail, an incident, place or person...

The Process- Part I

1.Write what you remember:

2. Can you figure out what led you to remember this particular place, time or person?

Our human mind remembers what is different from our normal routine. When marketing a product, experts focus on what makes the product different from the rest. Designs and ad campaigns are created around these qualities. What makes you stand out in a crowd? That difference is the very quality sure to bring customers to your door. The customers will remember you and tell others. The following process will help you determine what makes you different from the others in your field.

The Process- Part II

1. Put yourself in your customer's shoes. What is the first thing you notice when you walk into your establishment?

Take a moment and become comfortable. Relax and breathe deeply. Once you have cleared your mind, answer these questions as quickly as possible.

2. Compare yourself to others in your field. How are you different?

3. Look at the qualities you've listed, are they positive, desirable qualities? How would you describe them (colors, textures, value)?

4. Write a statement, in one sentence, about what makes you different.

Your differences are valuable to your work. These qualities give rich variety and need to be emphasized in your logo and marketing plans. Remember the strip show owner? His differences are that his is a family business (unusual in his particular field), and he truly desires to help his customers reduce their stress. With this positive purpose in mind, the door is open to many possibilities for meeting his goals in a more expansive way.

Chapter Four

Who are Your Customers?

"The big 'C' means caring, concern, clear communication for customers"

The needs and desires of people are changing. Although there are still constant basic needs, the marketplace is more global. What we do affects everyone in the Universe. People have become more concerned with the environment and humanistic endeavors. There are many reasons. The world and its economy are more connected through advances in technology, like the Internet. The earth and its atmosphere are showing undeniable effects of pollutants.

Other factors in the consumer marketplace are attitude changes about health care. People are beginning to take a more "self-responsible" approach to health; better eating habits and more exercise. Also there is a larger population of "baby boomers" living healthier, longer, more productive lives, as well as those seniors who need extensive health care facilities.

When creating your logo, the first concern is your customer. The logo design reflects your purpose, incorporates your vision of the future, is a tool for your mission, and finally, ***attracts*** your target customer. Who is your customer? What are their buying habits? What are their desires? These are important questions, and when answered can focus your marketing efforts wisely.

Your customer description can begin with the help of the following chart created by and for advertising agencies:

Six American Types

1. Traditionalists:

Midwest values, 60% blue collar

#1 VALUE: Family

They get together on weekends, not out to change the world, shop at Sears, Wal-Mart, etc., Do not like change.

Attracted by low cost.

2. Emulators:

Young, they model successful people

#1 VALUE: Confidence

They are motivated, sex driven, materialistic, confused, want to be somebody.

Attracted by mystery!

3. Movers & Shakers:

#1 in their field, know they are best

Earn $100,000 a year

#1 VALUE: They are unique

They are heads of companies & entrepreneurs

Attracted by creativity and ingenuity, they do not want to be one of the pack!

4. Do Gooders:

Mission oriented, good people, outdoorsy

#1 VALUE: Intelligent

Environmental concerns, poor & homeless concerns, don't like government programs mostly college graduates, #1: long hair,

VW bus, #2: got into system, changes from within, drives an intelligent car, i.e.. Volvo. *Attracted by environmental and social issues, does not want to be seduced by the system! New thought.*

5. Health Minded:

Usually over 40 years in age, retired or independent, extra time

#1 VALUE: Health Conscious

Free to travel, volunteer, do workshops, support the Arts, fixed income, buy travel vehicles, gifts for grandchildren. *Attracted by health issues, travel, stocks and investments.*

6. Needy:

Poor, on welfare, no advertising, served by nonprofit groups & government support.

Take a few moments and relax. Clear your mind through deep breathing and begin to answer these questions as quickly as possible.

The Process

1. Contemplate the Six American Types and write which qualities most probably fit your customers.

2. Can your product or service be used by people around the world? How does it help them?

3. Describe your global customer using qualities like the American Types chart. How does the American customer differ from the global customer?

4.. Write a statement, in one sentence, describing your target market.

Our strip show bar owner might consider a wider customer base through changing how he accomplishes his business purpose. This can be accomplished by looking at how his entertainment programs can be broadened.

Chapter Five

Show Me... a Creative Process

"At the core of every person rests creativity beyond our comprehension"

You have peeled the apple skin, carved the fruit, and exposed "seeds for growth." We are now ready to carve further into the seed. Within this tiny bit of shiny dark seed is all that is needed to create a huge apple tree. A most powerful and mysterious force is at work, for the idea of the tree, its fruit and the intricate engineering knowledge to create it is stored here. This type of "creativity" rests within every human being as well. In this chapter you will be exploring your creative potential as the process of designing your logo begins.

Most people think they are not creative. Somewhere during their lifetime someone has criticized them for being different, laughed at their efforts in music, art or dance; or an authority figure has made an example of their supposed creative inadequacies. When we are criticized we often close a door inside ourselves that may not ever be opened. Many times we carry these "old ideas' with us into every phase of our lives. In the business world it becomes a fear of being different, which is the very quality that can bring success. Creativity does eventually enhance the bottom line.

While pursuing my Masters degree in Biomedical Illustration, I spent four years in premedical studies and the study of human anatomy.

I discovered many astonishing characteristics of the human body and the way it works. One of the most incredible findings is the difference between the left and right side of the brain. The functions of the right and left brain show that every human has the capacity for immense creativity. The block to expressing new ideas is our own (and that of society's) reluctance to accept change. Each of us has innate creative ability that can be used when we change our attitudes about our capabilities.

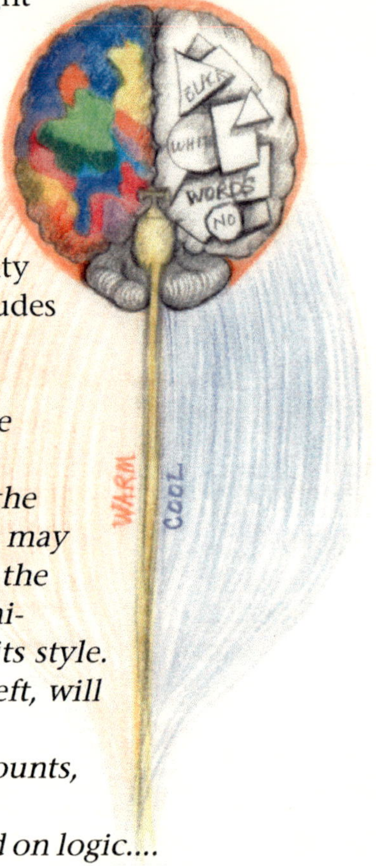

Betty Edwards, in her book, *Drawing on the Right Side of the Brain,* says...
"...as each of our hemispheres gathers in the same information, each half of our brains may handle the information in different ways: the task may be divided between the two hemispheres, each handling the part suited to its style. Or one hemisphere, often the dominant left, will 'take over' and inhibit the other half.
The left hemisphere analyzes, abstracts, counts, marks time, plans step by step procedures, verbalizes, makes rational statements based on logic....

"On the other hand, we have a second way of knowing: the right hemisphere mode. We 'see' things in this mode that may be imaginary--existing only in the mind's eye--or recall things that may be real. We see how things go together in space and how the parts go together to make up a whole. Using the right hemisphere, we understand metaphors, we dream, we use new combinations of ideas. And using the right hemisphere we are able to draw pictures of our perceptions."

Dr. Roger Sperry of the California Institute of Technology says...
"The main theme to emerge... is that there appears to be two modes of thinking, verbal and nonverbal, represented rather separately in left and right hemispheres, respectively, and our educational system, as well as science in general, tends to neglect the nonverbal form of intellect. What it comes down to is that modern society discriminates against the right hemisphere."

Jerre Levy, researcher in "split-brain studies at Cal Tech, says...
"The data indicates that the mute, right hemisphere is specialized for Gestalt perception, being primarily a synthesist in dealing with information input. The speaking, left hemisphere, in contrast, seems to operate in a more logical, analytic, computerlike fashion. Its language is inadequate for the rapid complex synthesis achieved by the mute, right hemisphere."

As research has shown, our creative, quiet, right side of the brain is filled with untapped, rapid complex abilities. Below is the different modes of operation in right and left hemispheres of the brain.

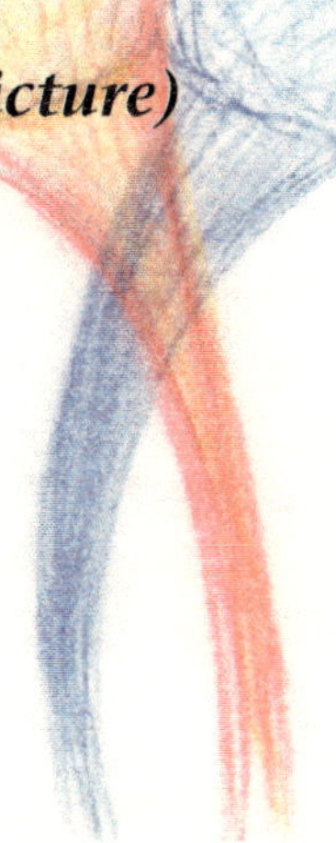

Right-*(sees whole picture)*

Speaks with pictures
CREATIVITY CENTER
Sees in color
Feelings
Acceptance
Inventions
Timelessness
Freedom
Dreams
Leadership
Genius
Intuition
Spontaneous
Vision
Wisdom
New ideas
Love

Left-*(sees details)*

Speaks with words
STORES INFORMATION
Sees in black & white
Thoughts
Judgement
Engineering
Time
Limits
Realism
Management
Learning
Logic
Planned
Mission
Knowledge
Old ideas
Fear

Balance between the two hemispheres is desirable for wholistic functioning. Ways to reach this is through more listening instead of talking, creating pictures through art, creative writing, music and dance. Through these activities you will open doors to new ideas and the genius that lies waiting to be used.

It is important to make the left to right brain shift before attempting design work and new marketing ideas. Some of the main ideas stored in the left hemisphere is "I can't do it," "I'm not good enough," and other self-defeating ideas still retained from childhood incidents. This is why it's so imperative to clear out mind chatter, become quiet and relaxed to open your creative side. *At the core of every person rests creativity beyond our comprehension.*

The creative response is spontaneous, present in the moment, is timeless and measureless. It comes directly from the genius part of you and knows only possibilities. True creativity shows no judgement, only constructive ideas.

To switch from left brain thinking into the creative right brain, you first need to setup your environment. To quiet the over active left mode, keep it occupied or confused. Listening to soothing instrumental music quiets the left mode. Drawing pictures is the best way to open to your creative side. The language of the right side is visual images and it knows how to draw. Too quick for words; its functional ability silently speaks through feelings as you create shapes and color. It is time to "open your doors to creativity."

1. Basically there are two types of colors: warm and cool. Warm colors are yellow-based, like the sun, and cool colors are blue-based, like the sky on a clear day. When you place a warm color next to a cool color, the colors vibrate. This creates an exciting balance.

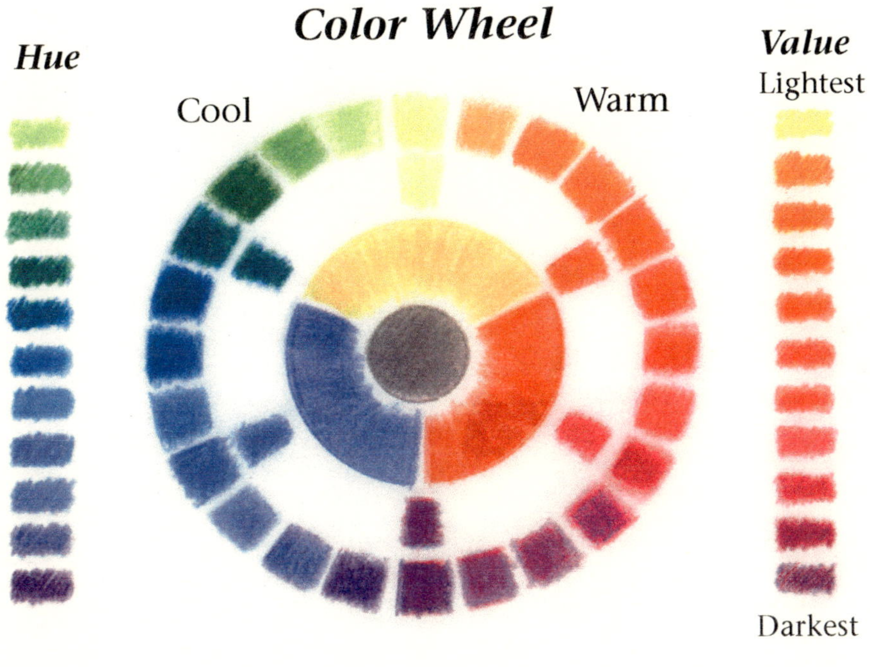

Shapes lying against each other create composition. Shapes either come forward or recede. Those that come forward are positive shapes, and those that recede are negative shapes. A picture is a balance of positive and negative shapes inside edges of paper, canvas, wood, or any other material.

32

Within the edges, shapes fill the entire space. They are in graded tones that range from the darkest area of color to the lightest area of color (value).

Value of Color- amount of dark to light

Intensity of Color- amount of pure color pigment

Relax for a moment and begin to listen to the music. Focus all of your attention on the music. When you begin the art process, allow your creative side total freedom by concerning yourself with the colors of the shapes, not what the shapes are.

When using your pencils, there are many easy strokes you can use. Find what is most comfortable as you are creating your shapes. The following are my favorites:

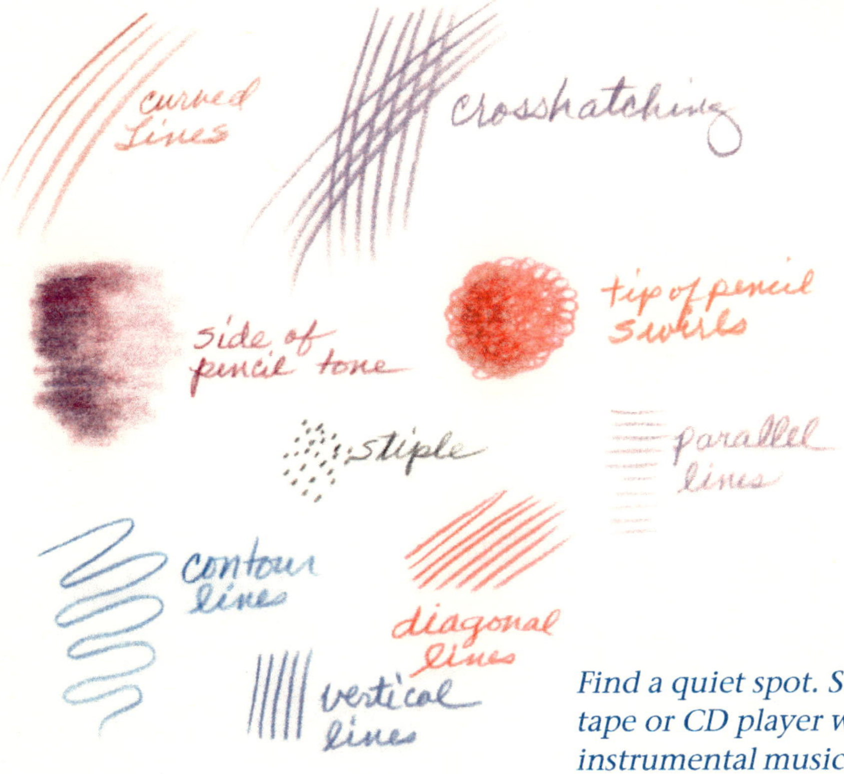

Find a quiet spot. Setup a tape or CD player with instrumental music and begin playing it. Before you on a table, place this book and a box of colored pencils. Quiet your mind by focusing on your breath. Breathe deeply and when you are ready, begin the process.

Open your box of colors, turn to the next page and begin to create warm color shapes next to cool color shapes inside the edges of the paper. Remember to fill the whole page.

2. Now start over with the same process. ***This time place the idea of your vision in your mind*** and create shapes while listening to the music. Do not try to analyze what you are doing. Keep your mind occupied with color, shapes and music.

3. You have now traveled into the part of your mind where creative ideas silently rest. The creative side of you is a *landscape of ideas,* mind pictures that fit together in a meaningful, colorful pattern. Take a few minutes and write how you feel about this experience.

4. Write any new ideas that have surfaced in the space below.

Chapter Six

An Idea Becomes Tangible

"A new way of seeing the whole picture"

A feeling of well-being, timelessness and joy comes through the creative process. Often I sit at my drawing board with a company's vision statement in my head and time disappears as I sketch out ideas that appear from seemingly nowhere. The creative response can bring a new way of dealing with every day problems as well. Your approach to life becomes more optimistic, displacing stress, anxiety and worry.

Leadership is a quality of the creative right side of the brain, while management is a logical left side ability. This is because the creative side is specialized in Gestalt perception: seeing the ***whole*** picture much faster than the logical left side can formulate a word. The left side is better at parts of the picture, orchestrating schedules and time lines; in other words, linear thinking. As you might have already surmised, our entire American system is based on left brain thinking; which leaves out creative thinking, true leadership and the holistic perspective.

Throughout this book we have been working from the inside-out. Bringing your creative ideas out to become tangible and useful. Stephen R. Covey, in his best selling book, *The 7 Habits of Highly Effective People*, says: *"Inside-out means to start first with the self; even more fundamentally, to start with the most inside part of self--with your paradigms, your character, and your motives.... Inside-out is a process--a continuing process of renewal based on the natural laws that govern human growth and progress.*

It's an upward spiral of growth that leads to progressively higher forms of responsible independence and effective interdependence."

40

Interdependence is a step into the leadership role. It involves a frame of mind that constantly seeks mutual benefits in all human interactions. Interdependence means Win/Win solutions where everyone feels good about a decision and committed to the action plan. This involves cooperation, not competition: it's not your way or my way, it's a combined creation, new way of seeing. This is called synergy.

During the creative process suggested in the previous chapter, you experienced the left to right brain shift. In doing so you have already changed your way of "seeing" to a new, higher level. The creative way of "seeing" is one of shapes and colors, no judgement as to merit, the "good or bad" of it. As this becomes a way of life, your vision becomes clear and encompasses the whole picture- a global perspective. This is the role of leadership; a way to accept and claim change as an avenue for growth. The following is a general way to practice a new level of "seeing."

1. Practice seeing without judgement, without stereotyping and assuming.

2. Look at objects with "new eyes," as if for the first time. Notice lights and darks, colors, both dull and bright.

3. Study the relationship of common shapes without thinking "it should look a certain way."

These ways of seeing will keep your creativity available at all times, and you will be able to have more of your ideas become tangible.

Chapter Seven

A Landscape of Ideas

"Imagine ideas that fit within the total picture, ideas that touch everything."

Each part of each picture you've created is important to the total design; if you remove a part, the whole is changed. The same is true of ideas. Each idea you have is part of a bigger picture, so every idea is important and touches each other idea in some way.

A landscape of ideas floods through your mind after you have unlocked and opened your creative doors. The right side of the brain is a master at seeing the whole picture, so at this point go back to the pictures you created earlier. First of all, relax and breath deeply.

The Process

1. Look at the pictures carefully.
2. Do you see a consistent theme in them? (Color consistency, distinctive shapes, a certain feeling or an overall concept). Write down what this tells you.

3. Make three small thumbnail sketches of the ideas that mean the most to you.

Each of your rough ideas has a theme behind it, a certain direction. These examples show a marketing theme for our strip show owner:

Idea #1

Expansion into traditional music to attract a family audience, some storytelling for children

Idea #2

Vaudeville/ Follies theme--attracts older crowd, with more leisure time, male & female

Idea #3

Stay with business people, expand to both male & female, add fashion shows/models at lunch & dinner

Our strip show bar owner can expand his customer base by supplying entertainment for both male and female, children and seniors. This will fulfill his purpose of "reducing stress in a relaxing atmosphere" in a more wholistic way. Of course, in order to attract this type of market he will need to "let go" of past ways of doing business, or change the strip show to a less limiting, *acceptable* diversion for the "male only" crowd, such as fanciful fashion shows. Example:

Each of the strip show bar logo sketches have different shapes; a circle, rectangle, triangle and free form. Different shapes attract certain types of people.

1. The circle: wholistc, earth oriented, intelligent, female, family types

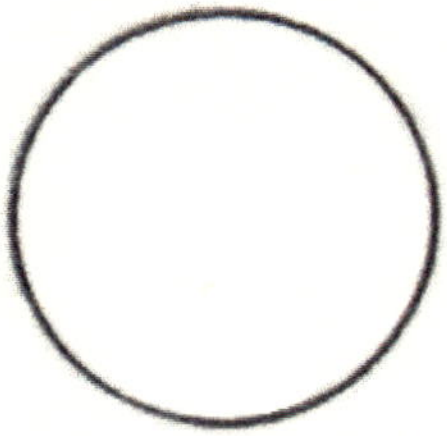

2. The triangle: power oriented, organizational, money oriented, historical, religious

4. Rectangle: Solid, male, institutional, technological, engineering

5. Linear: logical, knowledgable, management, structured

Vertical--upward action, growth, male, independent, Western

Horizontal--peaceful, traditional, female, interdependent, Eastern

Diagonal--energetic, change oriented, unique, individualistic

Cross hatching--synergistic, interdependent, couples, groups

These are structured, left brain shapes that can support a more creative shape with looser strokes and colorful shapes. When you add the creative side to these structures, the image becomes wholistic, balanced and attracts a wider global market. Some designers prefer the hard edged, flat color designs, with no tonal variation, that reproduce easier, less expensively.

I prefer the combination of both line and tone, as it brings a greater dimension to the image and impressions created by its form.

CORONA HILLS PLAZA

Logos can be created using:

1. Letters only
2. Visual graphic only
3. A combination of both letters (words) and image (art)

I believe that a combination of both words and art create true, wholistic communication. One without the other is less effective because the balance between the two elements is missing. Examples:

Letters only-

Bowen Ind

Art only-

Words and art-

CABINS
IN THE
LAUREL

Letters are left brained, black & white
Graphic images are right brained, seen through color

You can see how you are viewed by your customers based on the shape of your logo. If you are totally technical, you may consider a linear or structured shape; if you are serving the public, you would surely want a more humanistic, creative and colorful shape. If you are environmental or health oriented, a softer, more friendly shape is preferred. Stability requires a heavier, structured shape. If you combine a heavy, structured shape with a more humanistic image, the result would be a strong, viable image which shows with a commitment to people.

The following are different types of images designed with a specific message:

GUESTLINE

JoAnna's
ANTIQUES &
INTERIOR
DESIGN

International
Institute of
Iridology®

More examples:

APPALACHIAN

Evokes a feeling of unity, heritage and respect for nature.

CULTURAL CENTER

Catch the Spirit of Appalachia, Inc.

a nonprofit corporation

Both of these logos represent freedom gained through creativity.

Freedom to

Move

Dance

Sing

Body

Mind

Energetics

Chapter 8

Designing Your Logo

"Your uniqueness is your greatest asset"

A logo is a tiny design bursting with a big message. It speaks with a loud voice about your purpose and represents your future. It can add legitimacy and color the opinion of any product or service. To be accepted in the global marketplace, several qualities are essential.

1. ***Universal in theme***
2. ***Flexible for a changing market***
3. ***Effective when transmitted by fax, e-mail or on the Internet***
4. ***Easily understood, no matter what language or traditions***
5. ***Non-stereotypical***
6. ***Timeless in its style***

CORE
CORPORATION

Once you have considered all of these factors, the first practical design decision is based on your budget. If your logo will be printed on stationery, forms, and brochures, how many colors can you use? Each addition of one color will raise the printing fees 25%. You can use one, two, three or more Pantone colors. The four process colors allows you a whole rainbow of colors, and is 75% more expensive than one color. Would you like raised letters, embossing, varnishing, gold or colored foils. Visit you local printer to get estimates for each design element. If you would like a designer for your logo ideas, secure the local going rates. Once you establish a budget for your logo and support marketing materials, you can make informed decisions about design strategies.

Three and four colors can be incredible visually, and if designed for mass quantities, the printing price per unit can drop to two color prices. Small quantities can be reproduced economically on modern computer printers.

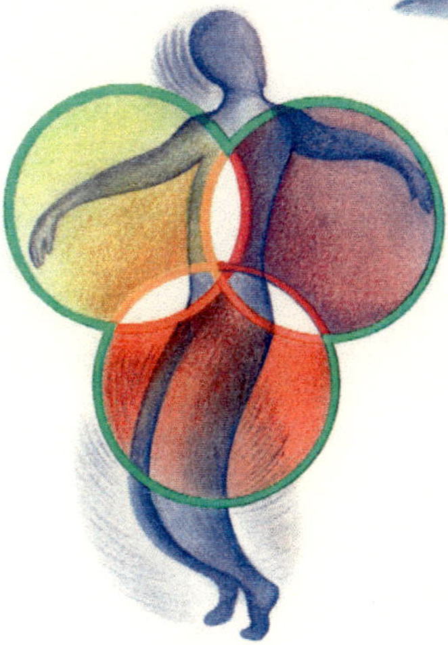

Two-color printing is still very affordable and is eye catching when using contrasting colors on a tinted paper stock. Warm colors against cool colors with combinations of screens and tones can create a visually appealing corporate package.

One color can be effective with the use of screens, halftones, along with 100% color on a tinted paperstock:

Once you decide the amount of color and special elements you desire, the design process can begin. This requires another decision. A collaboration with the right designer can bring extraordinary results when they become your eyes and hands. Either way, by yourself, in committee, and/or with a designer/design team, the steps are still the same.

Armed with colored pencils, markers and tracing paper, one sits at the design board (or computer) and begins sketching, with purpose, vision and mission in mind. Again, play soothing instrumental music, relax, and make the left to right brain switch, where the experience of creativity is timeless. Frank Lloyd Wright, Architect, says in his book, “In the Realm of Ideas”... *“The song, the master-piece, the edifice are a warm outpouring of the heart of mankind--human delight in life triumphant: we glimpse the infinite. That glimpse or vision is what makes art a matter of inner experience--therefore sacred, and no less but rather more individual in this age, I assure you, than ever before.”*

Sketching Process

Sketching is loose and free. Use colors as inspiration strikes you, yet base everything on an idea about your purpose, vision and customer. The creation of your logo is done in stages.

1. Consider the borders of the area you are sketching in. Do small thumbnail sketches concentrating on shapes, value and color.

Progression of an idea.

APPLE CORE PRODUCTIONS

Your thumbnail sketches:

2. Select the three most appealing thumbnails and enlarge those sketches so that you can begin to incorporate detail. Begin to add type that supports your graphic image. (Selection of a specific typeface will come at a later stage).

Enlarging and adding more detail:

Adding detail:

3. Allow your creativity to flow freely with colors, as you experiment with tone and intensity.

Positive and negative shape depend on value and intensity:

Develop value and intensity:

Repeat this process with three selected ideas.

Once you have sketched three rough idea/concept directions, take these ideas to your marketing team, corporate board, and all other interested parties. Ask for their valued and truthful response. Consider all options and opinions and return to the drawing board. Incorporate new ideas, for these ideas bring the wholeness that is necessary. By now you are getting closer to a finished idea. Again repeat the same evaluation process with everyone concerned. Usually at this point you become focused on the right logo idea for your business. Incorporate new suggestions into the agreed upon logo and complete a comprehensive design. This is the last stage before the finished artwork is created. Now you can call in a professional designer to take it to comprehensive and finished artwork, or complete the process yourself.

4. Comprehensive design:

5. Complete the artwork using materials you are most comfortable with... watercolor, soft pastels, colored pencils, paper, computer graphics, etc. I use soft pastel and colored pencils to complete most of my logos. I am comfortable with the technique and love the pure colors that are produced. The following is a brief description of my pastel dust technique:

A. Transfer the comprehensive drawing to bristol board paper (kid finish), using transfer paper underneath the sketch, and on top of the bristol board.

B. Now lay down a low tack masking film and gently cut around the different shapes in your design. I use a rotating Xacto knife, which allows me to cut curves and intricate designs. My purpose in masking the shapes is to create crisp, clear edges around shapes when I apply pastel dust.

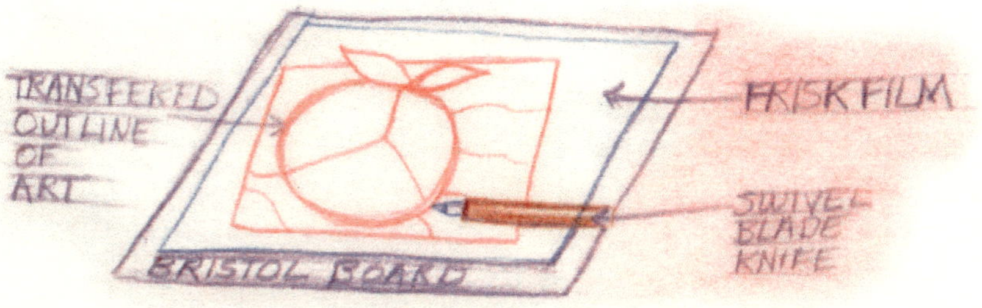

C. Remove the masking film from an area that is intended to be the darkest value and flake pastel dust onto the area using an Xacto knife. *(Do not touch the board with your fingers, your skin oil can smear the pastel dust. I use a piece of paper on which to lay my hand.)* Use a large cotton roll to rub the color into the board. Practice until you get a smooth flat color. Continue this until all of your colors are laid down.

For detail I use finely sharpened Verithin and Prismacolor pencils.
Finished artwork:

This colored pencil technique takes practice also. For me it allows my creativity to freely change colors at any time and to combine many shimmering shapes, hues & values of color.

You indicated a particular way of incorporating a typestyle. Now is the time to select a specific typestyle at the rough stage of the logo. There are hundreds of typefaces, each with characteristics that make them unique. Basically they are categorized by serif, (the small edges at the end of each letter stroke) and sans serif, a simplified letter with no serif. Whatever typestyle you select, base it on the artwork you've completed. It should complement, and at the same time, work together as one unit of design.

Colored pencil drawings:

Chapter Nine

Working with Designers and Printers

"Working together in synergy creates exceptional, high quality results"

Most designers have a unique and special quality about their work. If you are located in a large metropolitan area, you can choose from many different types of professional designers, depending on what style you need for your logo ideas. When you call in a designer, ask to see their portfolio of sample artwork. This demonstrates their style and professionalism. If their type of work will represent your purpose and vision well, and they profess to be timely; try them. ***Word of mouth is one of the best ways to find a good designer.***

When you see a logo you like, find out from the company who designed it. Usually a company will be glad to refer the artist to you. Local art organizations and libraries have design/art directories.

Working with a designer can be an exciting experience. The most helpful suggestion I can give is to keep communication lines open. When you clearly describe the look you want and your purpose and vision, most professional designers will work with you for the best design possible. This is the most rewarding challenge for me; it is wonderful to create artwork that truly satisfies my client.

Choosing a printer depends on how complicated your printing job is, and the quantity you desire. Shop around for quotes and always look at samples of their previously printed work. Again, if you see a brochure or letterhead you like, ask who printed it. Find out if the printer had reasonable prices and produced the job in a timely manner.

Make sure you bring a mock-up of the job you want printed when you go in for an estimate. Ask to look at their presses and find out how many colors they can handle as well as the types of paper they use. Ask if they prepare a keyline or proof of their print jobs for approval before the job is printed. Also, some printers will allow you to get a press proof when the job is on the press. Many times this has saved me from having a job reprinted because of color mistakes.

When you find a printer you can work with, they become your partner in the design process. They can make suggestions about how your design will work better with their equipment and ways to set the job up to save money.

With time and experience, your printed marketing pieces can reach a high state of quality, which makes you look better and attracts more new customers.

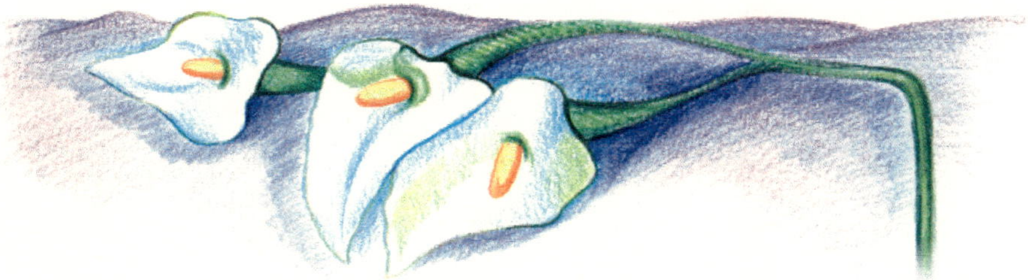

Chapter Ten

The Hidden Message of Your Logo

"A picture speaks louder than words"

AN exploration of your work has transpired on many levels throughout the first chapters of this book. You have taken its core and turned it inside-out. Deeply seated creativity has surfaced and brought a landscape of ideas to represent your purpose and vision. If you already had a logo or you created it in this book, it is now time to evaluate how it works for you.

If you had a logo previously, is it representing you the way it should? Are you proud to hand out your business card and know that the receiver will remember you? The following test can help you evaluate its effectiveness:

How Effective is Your Logo?

	Check one: Yes	No
1. Is your logo design based on your purpose?		
2. Was your vision statement considered in the design?		
3. Is color important in your logo?		
4. Were your target customers considered in your logo?		
5. Does your logo have both words and graphic art?		
6. Is your logo easily understood?		
7. Is your logo universal in its theme?		
8. Does the shape of your logo attract your target market? (Refer to pages 43-44 to review the types of shapes.)		
9. Is your logo non-stereotypical?		
Total	***Yes***	***No***

Refer to page 87 to see what your score is.

Shapes and colors have subjective meanings to everyone. Each person has a specific reaction to them based on personal experiences. We are not concerned with these individual reactions. The main focus in effective logo design is the universal subjective reactions of your particular target market. Let's start with colors:

Target Market--Female, 35-55 years old
Universal color preferences: reds, violets, pastel shades, deep yellows and greens, (blacks) *Blacks, greys and whites are not colors, they are values.*

Target Market--Male, 35-55 years old
Universal color preferences: Light blue, navy, forest green, and various shades of brown. (Blacks & greys)

Reds= Happy, energetic
Violets= Relaxing, regal
Pastels= Elegance, gentleness
Yellows= Bright, sunny, optimistic
Greens= Growth, outdoors, soothing
Blues= Cool, confident, truthful
Brown= Earthy, stable, traditional

The senior and children's markets favor bright, pure colors, while the ***teenage market*** is always changing with the fads.

Universally, women prefer shades of color with more flowing lines and softer edged shapes, while men in business prefer more hard edged, flat shapes. More and more new small business ventures are women owned and managed. A big percentage of marketing plans have women as the target market, so softer more elegant logos are becoming more popular. Also, with the Internet, these types of logo reproduce exceptionally well on the screen. *Friendly, humanistic shapes and warm colors are the most universally accepted, and this is effective in our growing, global economy.*

Chapter Eleven

How to Use Your Logo

"Consistency, Consistency, Consistency"

Your logo represents you when you cannot be there in person. Its benefits (or repercussions) are out in the marketplace continuously sending out your message of purpose and vision. First impressions are *lasting* impressions! What if, for example, the logo doesn't represent you well. What do you think your potential customers will think? Your one chance has been lost.

A well designed graphic image is one of the best investments you can make. Its long term benefits are priceless. When you pass out your business card, send out your brochure, put up your sign and place your advertising, you will feel confident about your image.

Marketing is all about getting the word out about your product or service through answering the needs of your target customer. When everything is based on fulfilling the needs of your client, your financial needs are fulfilled. High quality marketing requires the "BIG C's":

1. Consistency, consistency, consistency
2. Creativity
3. Caring
4. Concern
5. Communication
6. Convenience
7. Courage
8. Confidence
9. Clarity
10. Commitment
11. Conciseness
12. Colorful
13. Crazy

I believe the most crucial part of marketing is consistency of image (logo on everything), colors, promotion, and message.

One way of keeping your message consistent is with a "slogan" or "jingle." We all remember slogans like, "Good till the last drop," "It's a Pepsi generation," "Just do it," etc. Consistency gives the impression of reliability and it sticks in the minds of people.

Consistent colors and shapes create a much stronger message than the written message, especially if the person has only a moment to form an opinion. People remember shapes longer than they do words, because shapes touch the "feeling sense," which is located within the creative part of the brain. Shapes bring up other memories of past experiences that can either be positive or negative. Normally, soft edges reflect a warm, pleasant memory. ***A humanistic shape usually has a more positive response for the consumer marketplace and hard edges lend a feeling of solidarity and confidence to the business climate.***

Carefully plan your marketing materials to create the lasting impression that you need for increasing your customer base and therefore the bottom line.

Examples of consistency in image:

Brochure Cover and Sign

Business Card

Strong use of color and shapes create a warm, positive "feeling sense."

Hard-edged design creating a response of solidarity.

BUNKER HILL
DENTAL ASSOCIATES

The following is an outline of my *Marketing Materials Workshop.* Each stage is in order of development.

Consistent, Creative

1. Logo (created based on purpose & vision)

Life Power
CENTER

Front Panel of Folding Business Card

2. Corporate Signature
a. Signage

b. Letterhead, envelope, business card

These materials should remain consistent with the signage and always have the logo as the main center of attraction. The logo will be what people remember, not the words and the details.

c. Brochures

Again, be consistent with the logo and company colors. Incorporate the theme of the logo throughout the brochure. An example is the strip show bar, whatever theme he chose he would emphasize in his brochure, follies, family entertainment or fashion shows.

Keep the wording simple, very little type and lots of pictures and art. People may not stop and read, but they will nearly always look at pictures. If the pictures tell your story and make the selling points, you have sold them instantly.

Always show how the customer benefits from your product or service. Use proven sales words like- discover, love, money, save, etc.

A brochure is the core marketing piece for most businesses. It communicates purpose, vision and mission in written and visual form.It brings clarity and the look of stability to your business if it is custom designed and produced professionally.

d. Forms & invoices

A logo on the envelope containing your business forms carries the your message throughout the business world. People are more likely to take your forms seriously when your logo is officially prominent.

Colorful, Creative, Crazy, Clear and Consistent

3. Advertising

The advertising world is complex. To hit mass markets, big budgets pay for top names in television and radio. Your advertising budget will determine your extent of advertising. The important factor is to tailor your ad campaign directly to your target market. If it's local, advertise tightly to a specific local area. This way your money is wisely used in a planned fashion, not thrown to the advertising winds.

Whatever your budget, be creative, clear, crazy and consistent. The idea is to get noticed first, then sell. Use your logo on everything you do. Also know that just one ad every now and then does not work. Your campaign must be planned and consistent. Each series of ads should run for at least three months, preferably six months to a year. The series of ads should play one upon each other, strenghtening the message with each insertion. As you can see, for advertising to succeed, much time, creativity, thought and planning is a prerequisite.

Forms of advertising:

a. Print--Magazines, newspapers, newsletters, outdoor billboards

An ad campaign involves many avenues of exposure. Picking the appropriate mix is an art form based on marketing research conducted for your particular market.

b. Direct marketing--Catalogs, display & editorial advertising, newsletters etc.

Direct marketing is a type of advertising that stimulates an immediate buying response through ad placement in print media and through direct mail. The customer returns an information response form along with a check, money order or credit card number for a purchase amount. This type of marketing cuts distribution expenses and can reach a larger customer base.

c. Television, radio

This type of advertising requires professional designers, technicians, video & film directors, performing artists and creative writers. Normally an advertising agency could handle this for you.

e. Internet

This marketing avenue can reach a world market. A wide range of new designers specialize in artwork for the Internet. Web page designers and other creative artists can be found through surfing the Web. Chapter twelve, in this book, will give more Web page design information.

Caring, Considerate, Concerned, Committed, Consistent

4. Public Relations Materials

a. Press Kit--folder, photos, editorial materials

Whatever is happening in a positive nature with your products and services can be of interest to the information media. A well designed press kit about you and your history should be sent to local newspapers, magazines, radio and television. A press kit contains professional photos, a fact sheet with "Who, what, where, why and how," a one-page press release about a particular event and a feature article of special interest to your community. This press kit should be packaged within a folder with your logo printed on the outside and your business cards and brochure on the inside. Trade magazines in your field of endeavor are always interested in product news and will usually print your information.

Public relations can be the most effective promotions you can do and it's free if you do it yourself. Get to know your local editors; take them out to lunch, and this will help to get your stories in the media. For large public relations campaigns a professional Public Relations Specialist can be hired for long term and specialized projects.

b. Trade show materials--displays, exhibits
Your logo is the primary graphic at trade shows. These shows are the places to meet others in your field, sell your product and meet your customers face to face. In some industries this is the event of the year. It always pays to be out there personally spreading the word about your business, handing out business cards and brochures.

c. Networking Materials--incentives, referral plan, educational and promotional materials (film, videos, CD's). Education about your product or service is a great way to make lifelong customers. When people understand your purpose they will accept it and become a devoted "word of mouth" marketer of your business.

In marketing you consider the customers needs and then adjust your product to meet those needs. You must always be alert to those needs through some kind of analysis or evaluation program. Considering the global market in your needs assessment is a wise thing to do.

5. Continuing Needs Assessment
a. Services or products that fill a need--continuous improvement
b. Service to as many customers as possible--always make your product or service as convenient as possible
c. Ongoing expansion of promotion with consistent logo identity

6. Challenging Sales Plan

a. Continuously reidentify your prospects
b. Get their attention with your logo graphics program and communications plan, including personal contact if possible
d. Tell your prospects about the benefits of your product or service
e. Prove your case through satisfied customers, case studies, etc.
f. Build value--show how much your product or service means to them
g. Draw comparisons
h. Build quality
i. Show the benefits by creating a vivid picture with logo, brochure
j. Make it easy for the prospect to buy quickly

As you grow, always have continuous improvement. Go with change! When on top, stay on top through consistency, concern and caring. Refinement is a part of change. Go back to your purpose statement, your vision and mission statement and update them. Ask yourself, do they still represent you at your current level.

Keep this book handy and look at your artwork often. Purchase a new copy each year and complete the process again. Check back through the years, and see how far you've come. You'll stay on course with courage, confidence and commitment.

Chapter Twelve
Your Web Site
"An Artist's Viewpoint"

The sharing of ideas, success stories and the multiple ways people solve problems makes the Internet a cornerstone of worldwide communication. From your small corner of the Universe you can access huge amounts of information and connect with others throughout the world. This creates an impressive advertising and public relations opportunity. The challenge is that you feel like a small acorn in a forest of giant oak trees.

On the Internet the art of getting noticed is the name of the game. Like the game of chess you make one calculated move at a time. The first organized move that is guaranteed to garner more clicks to your site is to create a great web page. The following design tips are based on an artist's perception and basic design principles.

The first principle I learned as a designer for multi media presentations, video, film, and television is to never use a white for a back lighted background. Light pours through the white space distracting from the main typed or visual message. It's also very hard on the eyes. Have you ever seen a white background on a TV show? You are advised not to wear white when you are interviewed on television. Yet when surfing the Web I see white backgrounds everywhere, especially large commercial sites. They give a busy, confusing look and are visually boring. On the plus side the information is usually quite good, so for those people only interested in words, these sites do well. For people who are interactive and visual a soft colored background is easier on the eyes and more interesting. A dark background works well when you want your type and images to pop out to greet the viewer.

Keep the layout simple and the images small for quick and easy loading. Use warm, yellow based colors against cool, blue based colors to create contrast and interest. To focus the viewer's attention where you want it, put bright warm colors in the foreground and receding cool colors in the background. Blues and cool greens are great background colors. Also to control viewer eye movement, put stronger dark to light contrast where you want the most attention. Use larger type in these important areas as well.

Make your home page sparkle with creative, strong, eye-catching graphics and the surfer may go on to read more about your offerings. Your logo needs to start the page on the upper left or right side. Organize your titles so that the viewer feels at ease and confident; consistency of design will accomplish this. Make sure your most exciting information is placed in the beginning to draw attention and retain interest.

Design each page in the 81/2"x11" format. People do not like to scroll down pages & pages.

Use unique metaphors when writing about your subject matter. Universal ideas with "today's twist" will hold attention and create a desire for learning more about you.

Continually update your page with news pertinent to the Web surfer. Keep a consistent look and feel to your page, this gives you a solid base for your changing site.

The second principle that will make your site a great place to visit is interactive design. Have places for people to type in their own messages. This input can be valuable feedback to you and others on the Internet. As you surf the Net there are thousands of ways to become involved with other people and their ideas. This is a "give away" environment. You too have much to give away. A newsletter can educate your potential customer and help promote your services as well. Strong, consistent, organized design will get you noticed and the interactive design of your site will keep people coming back.
A good idea is to sketch out in color what you would like your site to look like, write your copy and pass it on to a Web page designer. Local colleges have students who will put you site together economically. The technological knowledge required to setup your page using HTML language will take some time to learn. If you have the time, great, you can do it yourself with a good instruction book.

Once your page is up and running the next step is to advertise it. Put you Web address on everything- business cards, letterhead, brochures, direct "snail mail", ads etc. Use the Internet by placing well designed banners about your site and using the many opportunities to link with other sites. The best way to get attention is to design a Web page that is so great that it wins an award as a "cool" site. When you practice what you've learned about design in this book, you can create a site that is eye-catching, creative, interactive, unique in content, consistent in image and easy on the eyes.

the greatest joy in life,
is sharing with a friend

Appendix

Glossary

The following definitions are the product of the author in context with the meanings of this book:

Artwork. A finished creative work made to display form, beauty, concepts or unusual perception.

Composition. The harmonious arrangement of forms, spaces and colors within the format of a drawing.

Comprehensive Design. The artistic design of a concept accomplished after a number of revisions. This is the last stage of design before a finished piece of artwork is created.

Concept Roughs. A series of loose sketches that depict a particular idea or conceptual direction.

Continuous Improvement. Constant change that is in a positive direction. Always continuing to grow in quality.

Cool Colors. Colors that have a dominate blue tone. Cool colors range from lavenders to greens and any other colors that are bluer when placed relative to a warmer color. Cool colors recede into the background.

Creative Potential. The creative energy that lies resting within a living being. Within a seed rests the potential tree or plant, within the human being rests unlimited creativity waiting to flower.

Creative Process. Spontaneous movement that allows a continuous, intuitive flow of new formations of ideas, shapes, colors and/or musical notes.

Creativity. An infinite number of random combinations of ideas, solutions, discoveries, shapes, colors and musical notes brought into existence through a new insight and mode of expression.

Creative Response. A way of viewing the world through eyes of non-judgement, yet with discernment (the ability to see clearly) and co-creating with cooperation instead of competition.

"Big C." Communication qualities, beginning with a "c," that relate to customer service and marketing.

Direct Marketing. Selling a product and/or service directly through advertising placement and/or direct mail (catalogs, coupons, flyers, etc.).

Edges. In design, edges are the places where the artwork ends. Inside a drawing it is the lines of separation between the positive and negative shapes.

Embossing. Raising the space between two edges by mechanical means. Embossed lettering is raised higher than the surface of the paper.

Finished Artwork. A completely designed visual image that usually is composed of a highly refined piece of creative art. This is accomplished after a process of rough concepts and comprehensive designs that are refined to fully communicate a specific idea.

Gestalt Perception. The ability to see and interpret all experience, objects and situations as a whole, not describable nor understandable in parts.

Global Community. The realization that everything in the world is interrelated and a part of one whole community. When a problem occurs for one part, it affects the whole.

Global Economy. A worldwide economic web exists that links every economic decision and affects the entire planet.

Goals. Specific objectives set which include dates, amounts and places. Goals are signposts of progress within a more encompassing mission statement.

Halftones. A graphic image reproduced through mechanical means which creates a screen of tiny dots to simulate graduated tone from dark to light.

Hue. The characteristics of a color that give it specific distinction in the color wheel.

Image. A distinctive shape (noun) that is seen by the eye and interpreted by the brain. To "image" (verb) is to see an object that exists only in the mind.

Infinite. Existence beyond human comprehension, without measure; never ceasing, forever being.

Intensity of Color. The amount of color pigment (particles that reflect a certain color from the color spectrum that make up a ray of light) on the surface of an object. High intensity color has more pigment and low intensity has less pigment.

Interdependence. Two or more independent beings who are able to cooperate to establish a relationship beneficial to each other and to create something new, greater than its parts.

Internet. A technological link of personal computers to a web of information that connects with the peoples of the world.

Intuition. Communication from an unknown internal source that guides one to action.

Keyline. An exact reproduction of printers plates on materials to show what the printed piece will look like before it is printed.
Learning. Storage; ultimate use of ideas, knowledge and experience.

Left Cerebral Hemisphere. The left half of the outermost forebrain within the cerebral cortex of the human brain. Its specialized processes mainly deal with organizational and verbal skills.

Line. Linear, narrow strokes of a fine point pencil or pen which are print reproducible in solid 100% ink coverage.

Logo. A graphic symbol that represents the purpose, vision and mission of an organization, business or individual.

Market. An area where sales activity and type of customer fits a particular product and/or service.

Marketing. The promotion of a business (with a priority to serve the needs of its customers) through superior advertising, public relations, customer service, and a sales plan.

Mission. An action intention based on purpose that includes goal setting for specific results.

Negative shapes. Enclosed areas within a composition that recede into the background.

Networking Materials. Printed brochures, business cards, flyers, press releases, etc. that are used to personally pass to others in order to communicate and promote the purpose of a business.

Niche. The unique space where something fits perfectly, as if in a puzzle. In marketing it is where a business serves its customers with greatest results.

Pantone Colors. A type of color selection system for printers' ink colors that is universal to the printing industry.

Pastel Dust. An art technique that involves scrap ing soft pastel sticks to create a dust of color that is rubbed into the surface of matt textured paper.

Promotion. To make known. To bring to the public's attention in a positive way, an idea, event, product and /or service.

Process Colors. The four Pantone colors that printers use to reproduce a full color effect. Process magenta, black, yellow and blue, when combined, can create a full spectrum of hues, values and intensities of printed colors.

Purpose. The reason for being. Everything has a purpose for existence.

Right Cerebral Hemisphere. The right half of the cerebral cortex of the brain. It's functions include creativity, "seeing" the whole picture and relational connections.

Screens. Various types of dot and line patterns used to create special effects in the printing process.

Sketching. A preliminary, loose and spontaneous way of drawing that develops an overall picture with very little detail.

Spontaneous. An immediate response to a situation or idea. Being in the moment with authenticity.

Split-Brain Patients. Only a few dozen epileptic seizure patients who had a surgical procedure that separated the right and left hemispheres of the brain.

Synergy. A new, greater energy that evolves through the interaction of two or more individuals.

Target Market. A focused customer description that clearly designates where marketing efforts should go.

Thumbnail. A tiny, quick artistic sketch that describes an idea.

Tone. Ranging from dark to light in a drawing or sketch.

Value. Amount of dark or light in a color.

Vision. An image of something that is not present to the physical eye, yet can be seen in the mind. A visualization of possible future events.

Warm Colors. Those colors whose dominate tone is yellow.

Wholistic. Seeing and considering the whole in contrast to separate parts. Observing the relationships, purpose and value of all parts to the whole.

"Win/Win". A situation where two or more individuals consider benefits of the whole in contrast to individual desires. An event where all sides win.

Materials

The following artist materials are personal preferences:

Prismacolor Pencils by Berol
Essential colors can be found in the 48 color set. Prismacolors have a soft, smooth consistency, with a wax base. They are great for blending and shading.

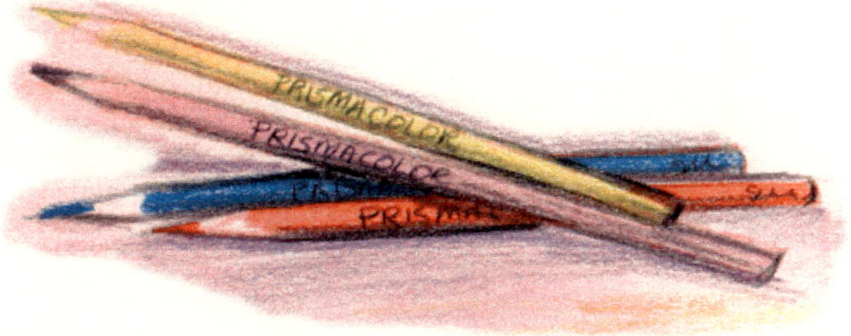

Prismacolor Verithin Pencils by Berol
These pencils come in the same colors as the softer version above, yet have fine, hard points. Verathin pencils are necessary for fine detail color work.

Soft Pastels
DESIGN, NUPASTEL
Nupastels are less flaky than other soft pastels and create brilliant, smooth color when using the pastel dust technique. Essential colors can be found in the 60 piece color assortment.

Xacto Knife
One of those essential tools for any drawing table. I use it for flaking pastel dust, cutting Fristfilm, pulling back the Friskfilm from the Bristol board and numerous other cutting jobs.

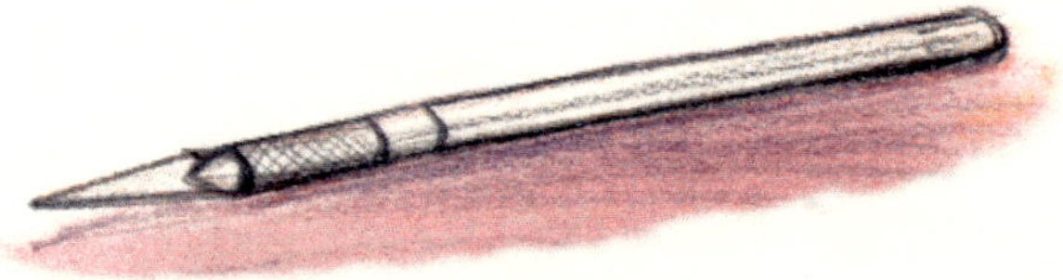

Swivel Blade
This knife has a turning blade that swivels to create gracefully flowing shapes when using Friskfilm.

Spray Fixative

Blair workable fixative will allow colored pastel dust (that is rubbed into the surface of mat bristol board) to be fixed into the texture of the paper. This allows many layers of color to be laid over each other to create a rich tapestry of color. This fixative is great for covering Prismacolor pencil strokes as well.

Erasers

KNEADED

A grey, soft eraser that can be stretched to most any shape. Will not harm the surface of the paper. Softly erases.

WHITE PLASTIC

Great for completely erasing.

Cotton Balls

Any brand of cosmetic cotton balls works fine for rubbing pastel dust onto the Bristol board.

Frisket Masking Film
A low tack (easily removed) airbrush masking film works well for covering areas when dusting pastel onto the Bristol board.

Where to order Art Supplies: If you do not have a local art supply store, there are many discount mail-order art supply catalogs. I find the prices and availability of supplies very good in the catalogs. The following are suggested free catalogs:

Art Supply Warehouse	1-800-995-6778
Dick Blick Art Materials	1-800-447-8192
The Jerry Catalog	1-800-827-8478
Artists' Connection	1-800-851-9333

Suggested Reading

Frank Lloyd Wright In the Realm of Ideas, Carbondale, IL: Pfeiffer/Norland, Southern Illinois University Press, 1988.

The Joy of Drawing, New York, NY: Martin, Watson-Guptill Publications, 1993.

The Drawing Book, New York, NY: McDaniel, Watson-Guptill Publications, 1995.

Color Drawing Workshop, New York NY: Borgeson, Watson-Guptill Publications, 1984.

Sketching School, New York/Montreal: Martin, Readers Digest Association, Inc., 1991.

Creating Logos & Letterheads, Cincinnati, Ohio: Place, North Light Books, 1995.

Letterhead + Logo Design, Gloucester, Mass: Rockport Publishers, Inc., 1998.

Drawing on the Right Side of the Brain, Los Angeles, CA: Edwards, Jeremy P. Tarcher, Inc., 1989.

The Creative Connection, Expressive Arts as Healing, Palo Alto, CA: Rogers, Science & Behavior Books, Inc., 1993.

Catch the Spirit of Creativity, Based on Creative Writing, Art, Science, and Heritage, Asheville, NC: Garza & Ammons, Bright Mountain Books, Inc., 1994.

The Seven Habits of Highly Effective People, Restoring the Character Ethic, New York: Covey, A Fireside Book, Simon & Schuster, 1990.

How Effective is the
Hidden Message of Your Logo?

1. Assign 5 points to each "yes" and 1 point to each "no."

2. Total both the "yes" & "no" columns and combine the two totals for one numerical score.

The following is an effectiveness chart:

Highly Effective---------45 - 35
Congratulations! Keep your logo out in your marketplace.

Moderately Effective---34 - 24
Great job! You may consider updating your logo to reflect your changing business and marketplace.

Marginally Effective------23 - 13
It is now time to update your logo.

Not Effective--------------12 - 9
It is now time to redo your logo.

Order form

Just fill out the form below and send to:

Seat of Your Pants Visual Media
10 Joy Lane
Waynesville, NC 28786

See our Web page at www.soyplogos.com for other products

"Greatness in a Nutshell" @$18.99 plus $4.00 shipping & handling(Total of $22.99 per book ordered.) Check method of payment:

VISA___ MASTERCARD___ AMERICAN EXPRESS___ CHECK____

Account No. | | | | | | | | | | | | | | | | |

Expiration Date: | | | MO. | | | YR.

*Signature*______________________________ *Date*__________

Name - As on Card ________________________________

*Address*_______________________ *State*_____ *Zip*__________

*Telephone*_______________ *E mail*__________

Total Amount________

I am interested in creative workshops ____
Design Services____

Doreyl Ammons Cain... Born and raised in the Blue Ridge Mountains of western North Carolina, she grew up drawing birds in the dirt of the mountain roads around her home. Even as a child she dreamed about being an artist, and painted forever in her mind the misty mountains she loved so deeply.

Later, in California, after achieving a Bachelor of Fine Arts and a master's degree in biomedical art, her dreams became a reality as she worked in about every artistic venue--storyboarding for films, owning her own design & advertising agency (specializing in logo design) while exhibiting her works of fine art in group and individual shows at the Smithsonian Institute, the Pentagon, University of Southern California School of Medicine, and universities, museums and galleries throughout the country.

Since coming home to North Carolina, she cofounded Catch the Spirit of Appalachia, Inc., a not-for-profit organization dedicated to honoring the heritage and creativity of all people. Through this outlet, she and her sister, Amy Garza, author and storyteller, have facilitated creativity workshops and performed (storytelling and spontaneous visual art) for children and adults in schools and colleges all over the southeast.

Today she and her husband, Jerry Cain, continue to design logos and brochures for business and have designed a new line of inspirational greeting cards and matted artwork.